KRISTA O'REILLY-

About Krista

In the past seven years Krista returned to school, started writing, launched babies into the world as she launched a new business, struggled with fear, anxiety and suicidal thoughts but also learned to ask for help and advocate for her needs.

She walked through surgery, chronic pain, and was diagnosed with an autoimmune disease. She has practiced embracing the truth of what she wants, learned to honor her wiring, and to shore up leaky boundaries. She buried several people she loved, said yes to adventure, worked really hard and gave herself permission to rest. She put down deep, strong roots of self-awareness and self-compassion.

And she picked up joy along the way. Enough to share.

Krista lives in central Alberta, Canada, and works as a writer & Joyful Living Educator. She helps "messy humans" like herself quiet the noise of perfectionism, comparison and fear to show up fully to their imperfect and beautiful lives.

Her message can be summed up in the following simple statements: you're imperfect; life is messy; show up anyway. She'll help you figure out how.

WHY SEASONAL JOURNALING?

It's human to experience ebb and flow in life. We move through seasons of transition and uncertainty; we tilt between self-confidence and self-doubt; we experience shifting levels of energy or productivity and changes in what we need or want.

We witness death and new life.

Life is messy. And beautiful.

Living awake and seasonally allows us to live grateful for the gifts in every season. It means consciously and stubbornly mining for these gifts.

Because there is wisdom knit into the fabric of every season.
Into the light and the dark.

Tuning into the season we're in – both the natural and metaphorical season of life – can help us live gentler, calmer lives.

As we notice patterns and rhythms of mood, energy, creativity, introspection, or cravings, we learn to better tend to our needs and love ourselves with less judgment. We become more attuned to and less fearful or resentful of the ebb and flow of life. We put down deeper, healthy roots of self-awareness and self-compassion that allow us to tilt and flex and not break when the storms come.

And we learn to mine for the achingly beautiful and sometimes heart-wrenchingly challenging gifts inherent in every season.

Krista xo

HOW TO USE THE JOURNAL

52 Mondays: Summer Session is meant to journey with you through 13 weeks of your imperfect and oh, so beautiful life and prompt you to notice what's happening in the natural world around you and in your inner world.

It is an invitation to read one short reflection as you start each fresh, new week and then to ponder or reflect on the practical application to your life as you move through the days ahead.

I have provided 3 journaling or reflection prompts you may choose to use to get your thoughts flowing but they are simply an invitation that you may prefer to leave aside.

I have left the pages undated and unlined as in addition to writing you may choose to doodle or sketch or Washi-Tape in little treasures you find that speak to you of spring.

Finally, at the end of the journal you'll find an opportunity to "rest, replenish, and review" as you consider the greatest lessons you've learned or what you've noticed about life and self in the past 13 weeks. This R&R&R exercise also asks you to identify what you need or want as you step awake and purposeful into fall.

I hope that this simple journal will surprise and delight you. I hope it serves as a gentle yet persistent reminder to tune in to the gifts of this season. And I hope that in even one small way you enter the next season stronger, more self-aware, or happier.

Krista xo

We're living in the grace
of an ordinary day.

ORDINARY

Birdsong greets me in the morning through the open window. Sunlight sparkles and dances off the spruce tree outside.

The scent of coffee and eggs entice us all to an impromptu brunch around the worn birch table. Laughter and banter feed us as much as the simple fare does.

We're living in the grace of an ordinary day.

It's sticky and warm, mosquitos hum, blinds are drawn, windows opened wide. Sprinklers sway to moisten parched grass and the big fat peonies that spill over onto the chipped concrete walkway.

Blue Jays squabble though there's plenty to share, cool grass feels amazing on dirty bare feet.

It's too hot to cook but a big salad and crusty baguette with salted butter fill happy bellies after a slow, easy day.

Neighbors greet each other, campers are restocked, the kitchen floor is perpetually sticky with watermelon juice.

Late night stroll as the air cools down, a glass of wine in the old Adirondack chairs.

Just a humdrum, ordinary day.

Pause & Consider

1. Have you ever noticed the incredible beauty of "an ordinary day"?

2. Small pleasures can make a simple life feel rich and abundant. What small things or experiences bring you joy?

3. What do you think about Seth Godin's idea that instead of wondering when our next vacation is we should build lives we don't need a vacation from?

There are gifts to be mined in every season.

You're imperfect. Life is messy. Show up anyway.

There are gifts to be mined in every season.

You're imperfect. Life is messy. Show up anyway.

There are gifts to be mined in every season.

You're imperfect. Life is messy. Show up anyway.

There are gifts to be mined in every season.

You're imperfect. Life is messy. Show up anyway.

The ocean makes me feel small.

SMALL

The ocean makes me feel small.

All the heaviness and grief I carry around with me feels lighter when I sit, feet buried in the sand, sun warming my body and all the broken places of my life, watching the crashing waves. When I close my eyes and listen to the ebb and flow of the water.

I feel small.

I remember that what I can see and touch and smell is only part of the truth. There is room for mystery. There is so much more to life and this universe than I can make sense of. And it isn't all my responsibility.

The ocean scares and calms me. Both.

My spirit is drawn to the water and invites me to be still. To rest. I understand its power – a force that extends far beyond my own will or capacity to make things happen or to fix things. I am powerless in its wake. And this calms me.

Not everything is mine to figure out or make sense of. Some things simply are. Maybe I can lay down the guilt and weight and pain – even for a short while – at the water's edge and choose trust.

Maybe.

The ocean makes me feel small. And this is precisely why it draws me.

Pause & Consider

1. Where in nature do you feel drawn to when you need to heal or be restored?

2. Are you in need of rest?

3. Have you picked up a weight that isn't yours to carry - or not yours alone?

There are gifts to be mined in every season.

You're imperfect. Life is messy. Show up anyway.

There are gifts to be mined in every season.

You're imperfect. Life is messy. Show up anyway.

There are gifts to be mined in every season.

You're imperfect. Life is messy. Show up anyway.

There are gifts to be mined in every season.

You're imperfect. Life is messy. Show up anyway.

It's all shockingly beautiful.

IMPERFECT AND BEAUTIFUL

I am fortunate to live a stone's throw away from the Rocky Mountains. No matter how many times I visit I'm awed by the beauty and grandeur of this corner of the world.

Wildflowers sprinkle the highway roadside as we head toward the foothills. Birch, spruce, fir, poplar and aspen intermingle to form a gorgeous canvas of light and shadow that makes me wish I were a painter.

Snow capped charcoal mountains contrast with vivid blue waters. Lazy mountain goats and white tailed deer, along with the occasional moose, elk or baby bear, meander where they will, stopping traffic willy nilly to the delight of first-time visitors.

It's all shockingly beautiful.

But if you stop the car and edge up close you notice the dust and bugs, the scratchy weeds and thorns. Those wild animals are not as friendly as one might think and where there's a baby bear, mama is not far behind.

When you zoom in you remember that the micro details of life are not always lovely, comfortable, or safe.

Yet they work in concert to form a breathtaking whole.

Imperfect and beautiful.

Pause & Consider

1. Is it hopeful to view the details of life as tiny threads of a majestic whole?

2. Consider how choosing to see life as imperfect and beautiful might open the door to greater peace and joy in your life.

3. What medium or environment most inspires you or helps you hear/see truth?

There are gifts to be mined in every season.

You're imperfect. Life is messy. Show up anyway.

There are gifts to be mined in every season.

You're imperfect. Life is messy. Show up anyway.

There are gifts to be mined in every season.

You're imperfect. Life is messy. Show up anyway.

There are gifts to be mined in every season.

You're imperfect. Life is messy. Show up anyway.

Remember.

You're walking in the hope of your yesterday.

REMEMBER

This is what you dreamed about in years and moments past when you wondered if wishes ever come true.

This is what you hoped for when you were still afraid and unsure you had the strength or tenacity within you.

This is the life you yearned for and worked for and sacrificed for.

Remember.

When you feel pulled in one too many directions and you crave sleeping through the night.

When the kids are fighting and the house is messy and finances are tight.

If you're juggling projects and deadlines, pushing and striving.

Remember.

You're walking in the hope of your yesterday.

Pause & Consider

1. Gratitude can help us remember. Do you have a gratitude practice?

2. Adding a few mindful pauses into each day can help us check in, breathe, and choose anew the direction of our thoughts.

3. How can you loosen your grip and "make peace with messy"? Do you think this would increase your happiness?

There are gifts to be mined in every season.

You're imperfect. Life is messy. Show up anyway.

There are gifts to be mined in every season.

You're imperfect. Life is messy. Show up anyway.

There are gifts to be mined in every season.

You're imperfect. Life is messy. Show up anyway.

There are gifts to be mined in every season.

You're imperfect. Life is messy. Show up anyway.

If I numb the sorrow
I miss the joy.

WHY I LAUGH

Here is a truth I've learned for myself though many a proverb told me it was true.

Laughter is a potent medicine.

Summer is a time of juxtaposition. Cloud gazing and lightning storms. Days wading in the cool lake and tornados. Popsicles and mosquito bites. Flip flops and forest fires.

It's a season of taking action and permission to rest. Getting our hands dirty and celebration.

We wait for it and plan for it and sometimes wish our lives away in anticipation of it and forget there is no one season devoid of pain.

But summer reminds me to laugh. It reminds me that delight is interspersed with trouble. I can't have one without the other.

If I numb the sorrow I miss the joy. If I refuse the pain I don't bear fruit.

So I laugh.

I laugh at every opportunity that presents itself. I laugh freely and heartily like my life depends upon it. Because I think in a way it does.

I chuckle and guffaw and belly laugh deeply. I roar until salty tears run down my cheeks. I don't care what I look like or who's watching.

I'm busy filling up on life.

Pause & Consider

1. Consider if you want to make space for more laughter in your life.

2. Do you allow yourself to really live or do you hide in fear of what bad thing might come?

3. What do you need more of in this season of life?

There are gifts to be mined in every season.

You're imperfect. Life is messy. Show up anyway.

There are gifts to be mined in every season.

You're imperfect. Life is messy. Show up anyway.

There are gifts to be mined in every season.

You're imperfect. Life is messy. Show up anyway.

There are gifts to be mined in every season.

You're imperfect. Life is messy. Show up anyway.

Live awake
and aware.

THE SLOWER PATH

Efficiency and productivity are meaningless if we use them to mindlessly cram more in. If we rush through our days without noticing.

There are times I choose inefficiency on purpose because it slows me down and invites me to live awake and aware.

I haul up heavy loads of laundry from my basement and hang them on our old laundry line. They might get rained on. The towels dry crunchy, rough on my skin. But there is a methodical, gentle rhythm to hanging up sheets and pajamas, one corner at a time.

Walking with a little person is a lesson in joyful inefficiency. It's hard to get anywhere quickly with a small human - they stop to check out leaves and rocks, butterflies and interesting bugs. They invite you to join in their delightful process of discovery.

Chopping, stirring, simmering, and seasoning as I go slows me down. I pull out little bits of leftovers and get creative with them or play in the kitchen by figuring out how to use up the colorful, weekly veggie hamper from a local farm. Slow food is a happy thing.

Efficiency isn't everything and summer is a beautiful opportunity to take the slower path.

Pause & Consider

1. Consider doing a slow experiment: wash dishes by hand, hang your laundry, take the scenic route. Notice if this helps you live more awake and in-tune with the seasons?

2. Do you need to pad your days a little more so you're not always rushing?

3. Have you ever considered a "staycation" to explore your neighborhood or city with new eyes?

There are gifts to be mined in every season.

You're imperfect. Life is messy. Show up anyway.

There are gifts to be mined in every season.

You're imperfect. Life is messy. Show up anyway.

There are gifts to be mined in every season.

You're imperfect. Life is messy. Show up anyway.

There are gifts to be mined in every season.

You're imperfect. Life is messy. Show up anyway.

Are you consciously building
the life you want?

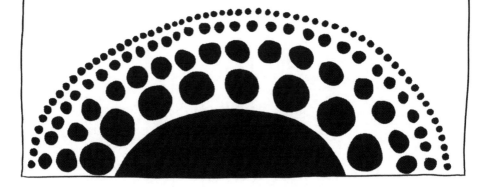

THE MARKET

Colorful bins of fresh produce, in-season, bustling crowds, a young busker playing his violin for a bit of extra cash.

I'm off on a treasure hunt to find the most beautiful bunch of carrots - purple, orange, and yellow, an assortment of deeply hued greens that make summer cooking feel like artwork - chard, kale, romaine, radicchio. Peppers, tomatoes, red pepper hummus, bagels and blackberries, fill my bags to bursting with possibility and colour.

Life can't get any better than this. I carefully select a beeswax candle pillar, pot of cinnamon-flavored honey, a small jar of spicy of korean kimchi - the kind my mom used to love, and a bottle of local raspberry wine. These treats will sprinkle more love throughout the week.

I inhale the scent of the popcorn and hot pizza, sold by the slice. Dogs and their humans of various walks of life sit around in clumps outside the market on the well-worn grass, under a canopy of green. And we smile and nod.

We mosey along the colorful streets to pause at a coffee shop for an Iced Canadiano before making our way back home, arms heavy with pleasure at our haul for the week.

It's market day.

Pause & Consider

1. *What habits or treats bring you great pleasure - can you infuse life with more of them?*

2. *Pause to notice the sights, smells, and sounds that speak to you of summer.*

3. *Are you consciously building the life you want?*

There are gifts to be mined in every season.

You're imperfect. Life is messy. Show up anyway.

There are gifts to be mined in every season.

You're imperfect. Life is messy. Show up anyway.

There are gifts to be mined in every season.

You're imperfect. Life is messy. Show up anyway.

There are gifts to be mined in every season.

You're imperfect. Life is messy. Show up anyway.

Holding space for the complexities
and tension.

LIVE THE QUESTIONS

I'd been duped. Hoodwinked. The wool pulled over my eyes.

I had naively believed that one day we'd arrive. We'd have acquired the right stuff - home, vehicles, family, decent employment - and we'd feel like proper, mature adults.

We'd have figured life out and feel secure and pulled together.

But that hadn't happened. We were still as messy and unsure as ever. Life was still as messy as ever.

One summer day as we walked around our neighborhood I realized the truth with sudden clarity and dismay: there was no finish line.

We were all just figuring things out as we went - bumbling along - doing our best. Making it up. Sometimes faking confidence or know-how until we knew better.

Maybe I found the secret to adulting that day.

Perhaps adulting is simply about learning to live the questions - holding space for the complexities and tension.

Choosing to show up fully anyway.

Pause & Consider

1. Has life turned out how you imagined - do you need to acknowledge disappointment even as you scan for the all the gifts in your life?

2. Do you agree that we're all just bumbling along? How does this make you feel?

3. What would you like your 20 (or 30) year old self to know about life?

There are gifts to be mined in every season.

You're imperfect. Life is messy. Show up anyway.

There are gifts to be mined in every season.

You're imperfect. Life is messy. Show up anyway.

There are gifts to be mined in every season.

You're imperfect. Life is messy. Show up anyway.

There are gifts to be mined in every season.

You're imperfect. Life is messy. Show up anyway.

Loss can scar us and also teach us to see.

THE WAXWINGS

The day was bright and clear. I sat in my little living room, chair pulled up close to the big picture window shaded by the Mountain Ash tree, heavy laden with orange berries. The sun flitted and sparkled as it pushed its way through the branches, spilling wavy patterns over my lap and onto the wooden floor.

My mom sat across from me on the couch. She was dying. Except in that moment, we still believed there was a chance. I'd always struggled with anxiety but when my mom was diagnosed I felt like I started unraveling; the earth slipped on its axis and everything tilted just a little to the left. I stumbled along, unsure if I would ever regain sure footing.

But there I was and it was sunny and the Bohemian Waxwings filled the tree just outside my window. My favorite bird. And for a moment I felt something stir within me. A flicker of happiness in the midst of letting go.

And it dawned on me on this simple day so many years ago, that joy and pain can coexist in a beautiful life.

I saw hope that day. It is the thing with feathers.

Pause & Consider

1. *Pull your heart back from yesterday and your mind from tomorrow and just be present here, in this moment and day. How does this feel?*

2. *Do you have a favourite animal that seems to "speak to you" or offer comfort when you need it most?*

3. *Loss can scar us and also teach us to see. If you've experienced loss, do you see differently now?*

There are gifts to be mined in every season.

You're imperfect. Life is messy. Show up anyway.

There are gifts to be mined in every season.

You're imperfect. Life is messy. Show up anyway.

There are gifts to be mined in every season.

You're imperfect. Life is messy. Show up anyway.

There are gifts to be mined in every season.

You're imperfect. Life is messy. Show up anyway.

I can let down my guard, soak up pleasure,
and have fun each step of the way.

IN SUMMER WE BEAR FRUIT

I always feel a little unanchored in summer – unmoored from the structure and rhythm which provide me a sense of safety and purpose.

In summer I practice flexibility and loosening my grip. I let go of micro-managing and lean into spontaneity - a lot easier when I can run around in flip flops.

Summer is also a season of outward energy that I find challenging for I am more comfortable hidden, in reflection or contemplation.

In this season, I'm invited to practice loving other people well, up close, and showing up for them when I don't feel like it, taking risks, and doing hard things. I've needed to learn to build, use my voice, and get my hands dirty.

Interestingly, summer also invites me into rest. Into the juxtaposition of activity and rest. Both/and.

Into leisurely walks and reading by the lake and taking naps. It reminds me that I'm allowed to rest and play, to be mindful and present. That I can let down my guard, soak up pleasure, and have fun each step of the way.

I'm more a true fan of spring and autumn yet in summer I stretch, grow, and bear fruit.

Pause & Consider

1. Which season do you feel most comfortable in - why?

2. Which season stretches you or makes you uncomfortable - do you see purpose in this?

3. Name the fruit you hope to bear in this season or the coming year. Create a vivid image of what life will look/feel/sound like when this desire/intention comes to life.

There are gifts to be mined in every season.

You're imperfect. Life is messy. Show up anyway.

There are gifts to be mined in every season.

You're imperfect. Life is messy. Show up anyway.

There are gifts to be mined in every season.

You're imperfect. Life is messy. Show up anyway.

There are gifts to be mined in every season.

You're imperfect. Life is messy. Show up anyway.

Today is a lovely day to choose to live imperfectly.
On purpose.
With joy.

LIVE IMPERFECTLY. ON PURPOSE.

Today is a lovely day to stop waiting for perfect.

A perfect day to stop deferring happiness until you lose the weight or get a better job, until your kids never argue or you find freedom from the habit that weighs you down.

An ideal day to stop waiting to take imperfect action until you figure the whole thing out, you're sure he'll love you back, the risk of failure is microscopic.

A beautiful day to stop holding your breath until life feels free of struggle, until you have heaps of extra time and the wind blows in your favor. Till things stop breaking and the laundry stops multiplying.

An amazing day to stop trying to keep up, stop moving the bar, no more procrastinating on crafting the life you want. Striving for perfection is exhausting and soul-destroying.

You're not perfect and it's ok.

Today is a lovely day to choose to live imperfectly. On purpose. With joy.

Pause & Consider

1. What if the only thing holding you back from loving your life and this day is the thought that life *should* be even better than it is or you *should be doing more or better*?

2. Do a brain download of all the ways perfectionism is at play in your life.

3. Choose 1-3 words that describe how you want to FEEL in your life - do a free write or create a mindmap to describe your life if you embody these desired feelings.

There are gifts to be mined in every season.

You're imperfect. Life is messy. Show up anyway.

There are gifts to be mined in every season.

You're imperfect. Life is messy. Show up anyway.

There are gifts to be mined in every season.

You're imperfect. Life is messy. Show up anyway.

There are gifts to be mined in every season.

You're imperfect. Life is messy. Show up anyway.

I want you to know you're never alone and
life is better tangled up together.

TANGLED UP

I want you to know that some days you'll be breathless with excitement and I'll want to know all the details. We'll dance silly together and I'll soak in your excitement.

I want you to know there may be days when you fight to breathe. When it feels like someone punched you in the gut and left you weak on the roadside. But I'll pick you up and brush you off and you can cry on my shoulder until you're spent.

And there will be days when you cry because life is so beautiful. You will be loved and at peace. You will live with purpose and courage and everywhere you look you'll notice something new to delight in. And I'll watch you, happy, and whisper a word of thanks for you.

I want you to know that there will be days you doubt everything you've staked your life upon. The earth will shake and you will lose your footing. It'll be hard to walk steady but what's mine is yours and we'll journey onward together til you're whole again.

I want you to know you're never alone and life is better tangled up together.

Pause & Consider

1. *Life is short. Are there people you'd like to tell how you feel about them while you can?*

2. *Receiving help is just as important as offering it; how are you at asking for or receiving help when you need it?*

3. *Brené Brown says our sense of belonging can never be greater than our level of self-acceptance. What do you think about this?*

There are gifts to be mined in every season.

You're imperfect. Life is messy. Show up anyway.

There are gifts to be mined in every season.

You're imperfect. Life is messy. Show up anyway.

There are gifts to be mined in every season.

You're imperfect. Life is messy. Show up anyway.

There are gifts to be mined in every season.

You're imperfect. Life is messy. Show up anyway.

I am well.
All is well.
All will be well.

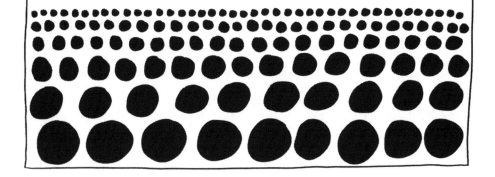

BROODING

As the leaves begin their turn to gold, always too early, I feel the subtle shift of atmosphere and a brooding of spirit that calls me inward, deeper into a space of solitude and reflection.

I notice a pull to forward thinking and planning and remind myself to slow down, to soak up the dregs of warmth and light and play.

The days are still long but there is a chill in the evening air now and I layer on a cardi and scarf and walk slowly, breathing, noticing, lingering - hungry for more sun and time. Just hungry.

Often it's only afterward, too late, that we realize we didn't pay attention. We rushed whole seasons of our life away.

I release the increasing tension in my shoulders and jaw and stretch my arms back to open up my chest. Another transition, a new opportunity to loosen my grip and practice curiosity. To make peace with change.

I am well. All is well. All will be well.

Pause & Consider

1. Do you have a guiding phrase, verse, or mantra that reminds you of who and how you want to be?

2. Observe your thoughts and feelings about change or transition or how it affects your body. What do you notice?

3. Do you have a tendency to rush your days or whole seasons of life away?

There are gifts to be mined in every season.

You're imperfect. Life is messy. Show up anyway.

There are gifts to be mined in every season.

You're imperfect. Life is messy. Show up anyway.

There are gifts to be mined in every season.

You're imperfect. Life is messy. Show up anyway.

There are gifts to be mined in every season.

You're imperfect. Life is messy. Show up anyway.

Rest

Replenish

Review

Consider the greatest lessons you've gleaned about life or self in the past 13 weeks.

Where do you notice yourself struggling or meeting with ongoing resistance?

You're imperfect. Life is messy. Show up anyway.

*Consider the greatest lessons you've gleaned
about life or self in the past 13 weeks.*

Identify what you've done well at and where you're proud
of yourself for how you've show up to life.

There are gifts to be mined in every season.

*Consider the greatest lessons you've gleaned
about life or self in the past 13 weeks.*

What do you most need or want as you step awake and purposeful
into the next season of life?

You're imperfect. Life is messy. Show up anyway.

BETSY HUGGINS

About Betsy

Krista has been my coach and cheerleader for over a year now. I found her at a time when I was searching for answers, and her words spoke to me in a very meaningful way. Through her incredible understanding of the human spirit I have started to recognise, and respect my own natural strengths and struggles.

I am not a writer, yet through Krista's writing I have learnt what it means to communicate. We all have thoughts and stories we use to make sense of the world, but we all also have our own ways of expressing these thoughts.
Mine is a messy mixture of making things, with lines and with pixels. Krista's words light a spark in my soul that inspires me to try to make sense of my own stories in a creative way.

These doodles you see in this journal are those. Expressions of thoughts and feelings that have been inspired by Krista's words. Simple, and honest. I hope Krista's words, and possibly my drawings, inspire you to go on your own journey inside, as I believe the gifts you will uncover are priceless.

With love,
Betsy x

If you want to say hello, I'd like that, I'm on Instagram @tinygiantlife

Made in the USA
Middletown, DE
27 August 2020